THE
TOTALLY
MUSHROOM
COOKBOOK

Printed in Singapore

The Totally Mushroom Cookbook is produced by becker&mayer!, Ltd.

Cover illustration and design: Dick Witt

Interior design and typesetting: Dona McAdam, Mac on the Hill

Library of Congress Cataloging-in-Publication Data:
Siegel, Helene.
        The totally mushroom cookbook / by Helene Siegel &
Karen Gillingham.
                    p.   cm.
            ISBN)-89087-727-0 ; $4.95
            1. Cookery (Mushrooms)   I. Gillingham, Karen. II. Title.
TX804.S47   1994
641.6 ' 58—dc20
                                                        94-2128
                                                        CIP

                    Celestial Arts
                    PO Box 7123
                    Berkeley, CA 94707

Other cookbooks in this series:
The Totally Garlic Cookbook
The Totally Chile Pepper Cookbook
The Totally Corn Cookbook

THE
TOTALLY
MUSHROOM
COOKBOOK

by Helene Siegel and Karen Gillingham
Illustrations by Ani Rucki

CELESTIAL ARTS
BERKELEY, CA

CONTENTS

"I am in revolt against the [domestic] mushroom of Paris, an insipid creature born in the dark and incubated by humidity. I have had enough of it, bathing chopped in all the sauces it thickens. I forbid it to usurp the place of the chanterelle or the truffle; and I command it...never to cross the threshold of my kitchen...."

—French novelist Colette

Hear! Hear!

Just as our tastebuds were craving something redolent of the earth and woods that could deliver big flavor with no fat and very few calories (mushrooms are 90 percent water), along came America's mushroom cultivators with an abundance of smoky, woodsy shiitakes, and delicate oysters to seduce and confuse us alongside those cute little buttons. Fine food distributors and quality producers such as American Spoon Foods in Michigan have also gotten into the act, packaging dried morels, shiitakes, and porcini accessible to anyone who has a mailbox.

So there is nothing for the proper American mushroom lover to do but gather up some choice morsels, head back in to the kitchen, and start cooking.

Most of the wild mushroom recipes here (with the exception of the morel and perhaps chanterelle preparations) can easily be prepared with white mushrooms or other wild varieties. They would still be delicious. What you get with wild, besides a steeper grocery bill, is some extra flavor and a scent that is a bit deeper or closer to the woods and soil where mushrooms naturally dwell.

Mushroom recipes are anything but finicky. Feel free to substitute mushrooms as they are available or as the mood strikes. (If you do decide to forage for wild mushrooms, be sure to have an expert verify that they are safe to eat.) They all cook in pretty much the same manner. They absorb other flavors magnificently and spread them around with aplomb. Whether you like your mushrooms wild or tamed, the message is the same: Cook, eat, and enjoy!

CONTENTS

MUSHROOMS
IN SALADS,
STARTERS &
BROTHS

HOT SHIITAKE SALAD

Here is a lovely light opener for a vegetarian dinner party. Don't let its simplicity fool you—the flavors are strong and sophisticated.

2 cups daikon radish sprouts
4 teaspoons rice vinegar
2 teaspoons soy sauce
1/2 teaspoon sesame oil
12 medium fresh shiitakes, caps only
    Olive oil for coating

Preheat broiler.

Divide sprouts into 4 portions and place on each salad plate. Mix together rice vinegar, soy, and sesame oil and reserve.

Coat each mushroom all over with olive oil. Place on tray and broil 1 minute per side, until soft and moist. With tongs, transfer 3 mushrooms to each salad, dark side up. Drizzle rice vinegar dressing over all and serve.

Serves 4.

MUSHROOM SALAD WITH TARRAGON CREAM

1/2 cup mayonnaise
2 tablespoons white wine vinegar
1 tablespoon Dijon mustard
2 teaspoons chopped fresh tarragon
    Coarse salt and freshly ground pepper
1/2 pound domestic mushrooms, thinly sliced
    Butter lettuce or Belgian endive
1/2 red bell pepper, slivered

In bowl, whisk mayonnaise with vinegar and mustard.
Stir in tarragon, salt, and pepper to taste. Add
mushrooms and toss to coat. Divide lettuce leaves
among 4 plates. Mound mushroom mixture on
leaves and garnish with pepper slivers.

Serves 6.

MUSHROOM & BROCCOLI SALAD

1 pound broccoli
4 ounces shiitakes, stemmed and quartered
3 to 4 ounces enokis, stems trimmed
1 cup thinly sliced green onions
1/3 cup rice vinegar
2 teaspoons minced fresh ginger
1 teaspoon sugar
3/4 teaspoon coarse salt
1/2 teaspoon freshly ground pepper
3/4 cup vegetable oil
2 tablespoons sesame oil

Cut broccoli flowerets into bite-sized pieces. Trim stems and slice into ¼-inch slices. Steam over simmering water until tender but still crisp, 3 to 4 minutes. Plunge into ice water to stop cooking and drain.

In large bowl, combine broccoli, mushrooms, and green onions.

Mix vinegar with ginger, sugar, salt, and pepper. Whisk in oils. Pour over vegetables and toss. Serve immediately.

Serves 8.

ENOKI

Also known as enokitake, these are the slender, white long-stemmed beauties with tiny caps that garnish many Japanese soups and salads. We use them more for texture and appearance than for flavor, of which they have very little. Always trim their woody stems.

13

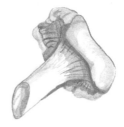

MIXED MUSHROOM SALAD

Sautéed wild mushrooms add a bit of depth to a simple green salad.

   3 bunches watercress, arugula, or frisee
   1/2 red onion, thinly sliced
   1 tablespoon balsamic vinegar
   6 tablespoons olive oil
     Salt and pepper
   2 ounces each oyster mushrooms, shiitakes (caps only), and domestic mushrooms, thinly sliced
   1 garlic clove, minced
     Lemon juice

Wash and dry greens and trim stems. Break into large pieces and place in bowl with onion slices. In small bowl, whisk together balsamic vinegar, 4 tablespoons olive oil, salt, and pepper.

Heat remaining 2 tablespoons oil in medium skillet over high heat. Sauté mushrooms with salt, just to wilt, about 2 minutes. Remove from heat and sprinkle with lemon juice.

Arrange green salad on serving plates. Scatter mushrooms over top and serve.

Serves 6.

BOLETUS EDULIS

The boletus edulis, otherwise known as porcino (or little pig) *in Italy, cèpe in France, and steinpilz in Germany, is considered by many to be the crème de la crème of wild mushrooms. It grows especially well in the Pacific Northwest. With its fat white stem, droopy brown cap and large size, it is unmistakable—both in appearance and taste— sort of like a mushroom by Disney. The flavor goes well with beef and all the usual suspects. Dried porcini (usually in pieces are available in the super-market.*

MUSHROOM PECAN PÂTÉ

This special pâté of sautéed shiitakes and toasted pecans is lovely with cocktails.

4 tablespoons butter
1/2 cup chopped shallots
2 garlic cloves, minced
6 ounces shiitakes, stemmed and roughly chopped
12 ounces domestic mushrooms, roughly chopped
   Salt and freshly ground pepper
2 tablespoons pear or apple brandy
2 tablespoons chopped fresh tarragon, thyme,
   or Italian parsley
3 tablespoons heavy cream
2/3 cup toasted pecan halves
   Juice of 1 lemon

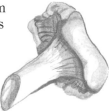

Melt butter in large skillet over medium heat. Sauté shallots and garlic until soft, about 5 minutes. Add mushrooms, salt, and pepper. Turn heat to high and cook, stirring frequently, until mushrooms shrink and give off their liquid.

Add pear brandy and herbs and continue cooking until liquid evaporates. Pour in cream and let boil until pan is nearly dry. Transfer to food processor or blender. Add nuts and pulse until texture has fine chunks and is spreadable. Season with lemon juice and salt and pepper to taste. Mix to combine and set aside to cool to room temperature. Scrve in a crock with toast or plain crackers.

Makes 2 cups.

Though gourmets may scorn the common supermarket mushroom, we refuse to be snobs where mushrooms are concerned. For us citybound mushroom people, domestics are always available, inexpensive, and easy to cook with. They are a wonderfully flexible ingredient for everyday cooking.

MUSHROOM QUESADILLAS

Here is a variation on the standard Mexican-American quesadilla.

2 tablespoons butter
1 garlic clove, minced
1/2 onion, diced
4 cups domestic mushrooms, chopped
1/2 teaspoon salt
1/2 teaspoon dried red pepper flakes
2 teaspoons lime juice
Oil for coating
8 corn tortillas
1 cup shredded Monterey jack cheese
1/2 cup grated Parmesan
Guacamole or salsa for garnish (optional)

Melt butter in medium skillet over medium heat. Sauté garlic and onion until golden. Add mushrooms, salt, and red pepper flakes and continue cooking until mushrooms soften and pan is nearly dry, about 5 minutes. Stir in lime juice and remove from heat.

Coat a medium cast-iron skillet with oil and place over medium-low heat. Place a tortilla in pan, cook less than a minute, and flip over. Sprinkle with about 1/4 cup jack cheese and 2 tablespoons Parmesan and then spread 1/4 of mushroom filling on top. Cover with another tortilla, pressing with a spatula to seal. In a few seconds, as the cheese begins to melt, use a spatula or tongs to flip to cook the other side. Turn a few times until cheese is oozing and tortillas are glossy and beginning to crisp. Keep finished quesadillas warm in an oven (200 degrees F.) while completing. Serve hot with guacamole and/or salsa.

Serves 4.

THAI PORK MUSHROOMS

This sweet and salty pork filling is great as a topping for noodles or wrapped in crisp lettuce or cabbage leaves as a snack.

12 large domestic mushrooms, caps only
    Butter for coating
1 tablespoon vegetable oil
1 garlic clove, minced
1/2 pound ground pork
1 tablespoon fish sauce
1/2 teaspoon sugar
1/2 teaspoon Chinese chile sauce
1 teaspoon lime or lemon juice
2 tablespoons raw skinless peanuts, chopped
12 cilantro leaves

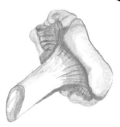

Preheat oven to 350 degrees F. Coat a baking sheet with butter and rub each cleaned mushroom cap with butter. Place hollow-side-up on tray.

Heat oil in medium skillet over high heat. Briefly sauté garlic, then add pork and cook, breaking up meat with a spoon, until it loses its pink color. Reduce heat to low. Stir in fish sauce, sugar, Chinese chile sauce, and lime or lemon and cook another 3 minutes. Remove from heat.

Fill each mushroom cap with a spoonful of pork mixture. Sprinkle with chopped peanuts and drizzle tops with oil. Bake 15 minutes. Top each with a cilantro leaf and serve.

Serves 4.

Since mushrooms are like little sponges, wipe them clean with a damp cloth or paper towel rather than soaking in water where they will absorb more water and lose flavor.

MUSHROOMS À LA GRECQUE

These tart little mushrooms are a standard French bistro appetizer.

- 1 pound small domestic mushrooms, trimmed
- 1 cup dry white wine
- 1/4 cup white vinegar
- 2 shallots, peeled and chopped
- 4 garlic cloves, chopped
- 1 teaspoon sugar
- 1/2 teaspoon black peppercorns
- 1 teaspoon coarse salt
- 1 tablespoon each coriander, fennel, and/or mustard seeds
- 1/4 teaspoon dried red pepper flakes

Place all ingredients, except mushrooms, in medium saucepan with 2 cups water. Bring to boil, reduce to simmer, and cook 10 minutes.

Add mushrooms and cook over medium heat 10 minutes. Transfer with slotted spoon to container. Rapidly boil liquid in pan another 10 minutes. Strain over mushrooms and let sit until cool. Cover and chill until serving time.

Serves 4 to 6.

HERBED MUSHROOMS ON THE GRILL

A nice summer accompaniment to steaks or chicken on the grill.

1 pound large domestic mushrooms
1 cup olive oil
4 garlic cloves, minced
1 teaspoon dried red pepper flakes
1 tablespoon each fresh parsley, basil, and mint
  Coarse salt and freshly ground pepper to taste
2 tablespoons lemon juice
2 cups tomato salsa

Trim mushrooms and wipe clean. In a bowl, mix together olive oil, garlic, dried red pepper, fresh herbs, salt, pepper, and lemon juice. Add mushrooms, toss to coat, and set aside 1 hour at room temperature.

Preheat grill or broiler. Thread mushrooms on 4 to 6 skewers.

Grill or broil about 5 minutes per side. Serve each over a pool of tomato salsa.

Serves 4.

DUXELLES PARTY TOASTS

¾ cup duxelles (see p. 92)
½ cup freshly grated Parmesan
⅓ cup crème fraîche or sour cream
48 ½-inch baguette slices, lightly toasted

Preheat broiler.

In bowl, mix duxelles, Parmesan, and crème fraîche. Spread about 2 teaspoons on each toast. Arrange on baking sheet and broil just until bubbly, about 1 minute.

Makes 48.

GRILLED PESTO MUSHROOMS

1 cup packed basil leaves
1/4 cup pine nuts
2 garlic cloves
1/4 cup freshly grated Parmesan
Olive oil
Coarse salt and freshly ground pepper
18 large domestic mushrooms, caps only

In blender, combine basil, nuts, garlic, Parmesan, and 1/4 cup olive oil and blend until smooth.

Brush mushrooms lightly with olive oil. Grill, cup side down, over medium-hot coals or broil under low broiler, 5 minutes. Turn, spoon pesto into caps, filling almost to top and grill or broil 5 minutes longer.

Serves 6.

BACON & CHEESE MUSHROOMS

Domestic mushrooms are great natural vessels for an exuberant stuffing such as this crisp bacon and cheese combination.

Butter for coating
1 pound (about 8) large domestic mushrooms
3 ounces bacon, chopped
2 garlic cloves, minced
2 tablespoons bread crumbs
1/4 cup grated mozzarella
2 tablespoons grated Parmesan

Preheat oven to 350 degrees F. Coat a baking sheet with butter.

Wipe mushrooms clean and gently remove stems. Place caps hollow-side up on buttered tray. Chop stems and set aside.

Fry bacon in small skillet over medium-low heat. With slotted spoon, transfer bacon bits to paper towels to drain. Bring skillet with bacon fat to high heat and sauté garlic and chopped stems about a minute. Transfer to medium bowl and add bacon, bread crumbs, and cheeses. Mix with a fork. Stuff a heaping spoonful of mixture into each mushroom cap. Place in oven and bake until top is browned, about 15 minutes. Serve hot.

Serves 4.

A MUSHROOM IS A MUSHROOM IS A FUNGUS

Brace yourself. Mushrooms are not technically a vegetable. Since they have no roots, leaves, flowers or chlorophyll, they really are a spore that in reproducing itself produces webs of filaments that fill in to produce "fruiting bodies" or fungus that people like to eat. Mushroom "farmers" raise these fungi indoors in huge, climate-controlled sheds since conditions need to be uniform to reproduce the same species.

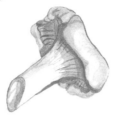

BROTH WITH MUSHROOMS, SPINACH & SCALLIONS

4 cups chicken broth
2 garlic cloves, peeled and crushed
2 thick slices fresh ginger, crushed
4 ounces shiitakes, caps only, thinly sliced
2 ounces domestic mushrooms, caps only, thinly sliced
4 scallions, trimmed and thinly sliced
4 cups thinly sliced cleaned spinach
1½ tablespoons soy sauce
2 tablespoons chopped fresh cilantro
2 ounces enoki, ends trimmed (optional)
Freshly ground black pepper

Bring chicken stock to boil in medium saucepan. Add garlic and ginger and simmer 10 minutes. Remove and discard garlic and ginger.

Bring back to boil, add shiitakes and domestic mushrooms, and simmer 5 minutes. Stir in scallions, spinach, soy, and cilantro and cook 2 minutes longer. Garnish with enoki, if desired, season with pepper, and serve hot.

Serves 2 to 4.

AGARICUS BISPORUS

The domestic mushroom, also known as button, white, champignon de Paris, or agaricus bisporus *was first cultivated in western France by Olivier de Serres, an agronomist to King Louis XIV. During the eighteenth century gardeners started noticing mushrooms in melon beds on the outskirts of Paris. By the time they were found sprouting in the caves outside Paris, they were the talk of the town. (Though judging by Colette, not all the talk was positive.)*

OLD-FASHIONED MUSHROOM BARLEY SOUP

Mushrooms and barley share a deep nutty flavor that is exceptionally satisfying. This thick broth is perfect for dinner with a crusty country loaf and a bottle of red wine.

- 1 ounce dried porcini
- 3 cups water
- 2 (14.5-ounce) cans beef broth
- 1 onion, diced
- 2 garlic cloves, peeled and crushed
- 2 carrots, peeled and diced
- 1 celery rib, diced
- 1/2 pound lean stewing beef, cut into small cubes
- 2 teaspoons dried parsley
- 1 cup pearl barley
- 6 ounces domestic mushrooms, roughly chopped
  Coarse salt and freshly ground pepper

Soak dried porcini in 2 cups hot water for a half hour. Lift out and strain, reserving soaking liquid. Chop porcini into bite-sized pieces.

Combine beef broth, soaking liquid, and water in stockpot. Bring to boil. Add porcini, onion, garlic, carrots, celery, beef, and parsley. Reduce to simmer and cook 15 minutes, occasionally skimming foam from top.

Return to boil and add barley. Reduce to simmer, cover, and cook 15 minutes, skimming foam occasionally. Add domestic mushrooms, plenty of freshly ground pepper, and salt to taste. Cook, partially covered, a half hour longer. Adjust seasonings and serve hot.

Serves 4 to 6.

AGARICUS BISPORUS (CONTINUED)

By the late eighteenth century cultivation had spread to Sweden and England so that now, in the late twentieth century, with companies like Campbells at the helm, the United States is one of the world's largest producers. (Russian gastronomes, who pride themselves on their steadfast love of mushrooms, scorn the domestic type. At times in Russian history, the wild mushroom has been a dietary staple.)

CREAM OF MUSHROOM SOUP

Of all the creamed vegetable soups, mushroom is one of our favorites since the flavor goes so well with all that silky cream and butter.

4 tablespoons butter
1 pound domestic mushrooms, thinly sliced
½ onion, thinly sliced
Salt and black pepper
3 cups chicken stock
1¼ cup heavy cream
1 tablespoon fresh chopped thyme
Fresh lemon juice

Melt butter in large stockpot over medium-high heat. Sauté mushrooms and onions with salt and pepper until liquid evaporates, 10 minutes. Add chicken stock, cream, and thyme. Bring to boil and remove from heat.

Purée in batches in food processor and pour back into pot. Bring just to boil and season to taste with lemon juice, salt, and pepper. Serve hot.

Serves 4.

WILD, WILD MUSHROOMS

If you are not the foraging type, the next best place to find truly wild, wild mushrooms is at local farmer's markets. You can spot them by the dirt still clinging to their grubby little stems and their less than perfect appearance. (Cultivated wild mushrooms, of which shiitake and oyster are the most prevalent, can be spotted by their cleanliness and uniformity. They are available at the supermarket.)

In the middle of the winter, at our local farmer's market in southern California, it is possible to find chanterelles, porcini, chicken of the woods, pied de moutons, an occasional truffle or morel, portobellos, an abundance of oysters and shiitakes, and several more obscure species— along with cooking advice from the mushroom man.

CONTENTS

MUSHROOMS &
THEIR FRIEND,
THE EGG

MIXED MUSHROOM TART

1 (9-inch) unbaked pie crust
4 tablespoons butter
6 cups chopped mixed wild and/or domestic mushrooms
3 large shallots, minced
2 eggs
1/2 cup half and half
1/4 cup dry white wine
1/2 cup freshly grated Parmesan
1/2 teaspoon coarse salt
1/4 teaspoon white pepper

Preheat oven to 350 degrees F. Bake crust about 12 minutes, or until golden. Set aside, keeping oven on.

In large skillet, melt butter over moderate heat. Add mushrooms and shallots and cook, stirring frequently, until mushrooms are browned, about 15 minutes. Transfer to pie crust.

In bowl, beat eggs with half and half, wine, Parmesan, salt, and pepper. Pour over mushrooms. Bake about 25 minutes or until almost set in center. Remove from oven and let stand 10 minutes before serving.

Serves 6 to 8.

MUSHROOM OMELETTE

2 tablespoons butter
1/2 onion, chopped
4 ounces domestic mushrooms, stems trimmed and chopped
5 eggs, beaten with salt and pepper
1/2 cup shredded cheddar or jack cheese
1 1/2 tablespoons chopped fresh Italian parsley

Melt 1 tablespoon of butter in a nonstick skillet over medium-high heat. Sauté onion and mushrooms with salt and pepper just until soft. Transfer to platter.

Melt remaining tablespoon of butter over high heat. Add eggs, swirling to coat pan. As soon as bottom sets, scatter in mushroom mixture and cheese. Reduce heat slightly and fold eggs to enclose, flipping omelette if desired. Sprinkle with parsley, divide into 2 servings, and slide onto plates. Serve hot.

Serves 2.

CHANTERELLES

Also known as girolles in France, where they are highly prized, chanterelles are beautiful bright orange mushrooms with an unusual upturned cap that reminds some of an umbrella blown inside out. They hold their shape well with cooking and emit a heady fragrance and fruity flavor often compared to apricots. Caps and stems are equally delicious and we like them best with poultry and game or in a hot bowl of risotto.

SOUFFLÉ OF CHANTERELLES

3 tablespoons butter
1/2 pound fresh chanterelles, sliced
3 shallots, minced
3 tablespoons all-purpose flour
1/2 cup half and half
1/4 cup dry white wine
2 teaspoons chopped fresh tarragon
3/4 teaspoon coarse salt
1/2 teaspoon white pepper
5 eggs, separated

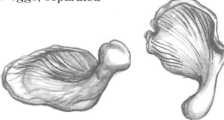

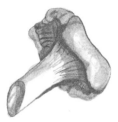

Preheat oven to 375 degrees F.

In saucepan, melt butter over moderate heat. Add chanterelles and shallots and cook, stirring frequently, until moisture is evaporated, about 15 minutes. Stir in flour, then gradually blend in half and half and wine. Stir in tarragon, salt, and pepper and cook over moderate heat until thick, about 3 minutes. Stir about 1/2 cup hot mixture into egg yolks, then return to pan and stir to blend. Remove from heat.

Beat egg whites until stiff. Gently stir half of whites into mushroom mixture. Carefully fold in remaining whites. Pour mixture into buttered 2-quart soufflé dish and bake 35 to 40 minutes. Serve immediately.

Serves 6.

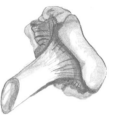

ASPARAGUS OYSTER FRITTATA

OYSTERS

The pale ivory oyster mushroom is thin-fleshed and delicate tasting. Both its stem and cap are enjoyable to eat and many chefs simply tear it into bite-sized pieces rather than humiliate its flesh with a knife. Compared to other wild species, oysters are rather bland though they are good carriers of other flavors.

8 ounces thin asparagus, trimmed
3½ tablespoons olive oil
4 ounces oyster mushrooms, roughly chopped
1 garlic clove, minced
6 eggs
¼ cup grated Parmesan
Salt and pepper
2 tablespoons bread crumbs

Preheat broiler.

Blanch asparagus in salted boiling water 1 minute. Drain, rinse with cold water, and set aside.

Heat 1½ tablespoons of oil in large ovenproof skillet over high heat. Sauté mushrooms and garlic 1 minute. Transfer to bowl to cool and wipe skillet clean. Cut asparagus into 1-inch lengths.

In large bowl, combine eggs, Parmesan, asparagus, mushrooms, salt, and pepper. Mix well.

Heat 2 tablespoons oil in same skillet over medium-high heat. Pour in egg mixture, swirl to smooth top, and cook until bottom is set, less than a minute. Reduce heat to medium-low and cook until edges are set and center slightly runny. Sprinkle bread crumbs over top, transfer to broiler, and cook until set and slightly golden, 1 minute. Cool in pan 5 minutes, then loosen bottom with spatula and transfer to serving plate. Cut in wedges and serve hot or at room temperature.

Serves 4 to 6.

CONTENTS

PARTIALLY
WILD
ACCOMPANIMENTS

POTATO MUSHROOM GRATIN

This low-fat gratin is delicious with any roasted meat.

Olive oil
1 rosemary sprig
3 medium baking potatoes, peeled and thinly sliced
1/2 pound domestic mushrooms, thinly sliced
3 garlic cloves, thinly sliced
Salt and black pepper

Preheat oven to 425 degrees F.

Coat a 9-inch square casserole or baking dish with olive oil. Lay rosemary sprig on bottom. Layer half of the potato slices over bottom. Top with half of the sliced mushrooms and half of the garlic. Sprinkle generously with olive oil, salt, and pepper.

Top with the remaining potatoes. Chop the remaining mushrooms and garlic, then scatter the mixture over the top. Sprinkle with olive oil, salt, and pepper. Bake, uncovered, until top is golden and crusty, about 1 hour. Serve hot.

Serves 4.

GRILLED PORTOBELLOS WITH OLIVE OIL & GARLIC

Large portobellos are substantial enough to serve as an entrée—kind of like a grilled steak with a lot less calories.

4 portobellos
  Olive oil
  Coarse salt and freshly ground black pepper
4 garlic cloves, minced
  Chopped fresh parsley

Preheat the broiler.

Wipe mushrooms clean and remove stems. Drizzle all over with olive oil and season with salt and pepper.

Broil about 4 inches from flame, gill-side up, 2 minutes. Turn over, sprinkle tops with garlic and a bit more oil, and cook 1 to 2 minutes longer, being careful not to burn the garlic. Sprinkle with parsley and serve.

Serves 4.

FRIED MUSHROOMS

Serve these battered and fried mushrooms alongside the kind of huge, charred steak they cry out for. You won't regret it!

    1 cup all-purpose flour
1½ teaspoons salt
    1 teaspoon cayenne
½ teaspoon baking powder
½ teaspoon sugar
1½ cups warm beer
    6 cups vegetable oil
    1 pound small domestic mushrooms, stems
       on, wiped clean

Combine flour, salt, cayenne, baking powder, and sugar in mixing bowl. Add beer, whisk until smooth, and set aside, covered, at room temperature, 1 hour.

To fry, heat oil in deep pot or fryer until 350 degrees F. (To test for readiness, drop in a spoonful of batter. If it bubbles immediately, oil is ready.) Dip mushrooms in batter, a handful at a time, turning to evenly coat. Then drop in oil and fry until golden brown all over, turning occasionally with slotted spoon, about 2 minutes. Drain on paper towels and complete frying. Serve immediately or risk sogginess.

Serves 4.

PORTOBELLOS

These are the sirloin steaks of mushrooms. Even the most skeptical meat eater will be favorably impressed by what happens to this thick, dark 4-inch disk when it hits the grill. It is a superb substitute for meat.

OYSTER MUSHROOMS PROVENÇAL

1 pound oyster mushrooms, torn into chunks
¼ cup olive oil
4 garlic cloves, minced
2 tablespoons chopped fresh Italian parsley
Juice of ½ lemon
Coarse salt and freshly ground pepper

Heat oil in large skillet over medium-high heat. Sauté garlic 1 minute and add mushrooms. Sauté until oil is absorbed, about 2 minutes. Stir in parsley, lemon juice, salt, and pepper and serve immediately.

Serves 4.

SNOW PEAS
& MUSHROOMS

    3 tablespoons butter
 1/2 tablespoon puréed garlic
 1/2 tablespoon puréed ginger
    8 ounces snow peas, trimmed
    4 ounces domestic mushrooms,
       trimmed and thinly sliced
 11/2 tablespoons soy sauce
       Freshly ground black pepper

Melt butter in large skillet over medium high heat.
Sauté garlic and ginger less than a minute. Add
snow peas and mushrooms and cook, stirring and
tossing, about 1 minute. Pour in soy sauce,
sprinkle with pepper, and continue cooking, stirring
frequently, 2 to 3 minutes longer, until snow peas
are still crisp and mushrooms wilted. Serve hot.

Serves 4.

CURRIED MUSHROOMS & CAULIFLOWER

  3 tablespoons butter
  2 cups shiitakes, stemmed and sliced
  1 onion, sliced
1½ teaspoons curry powder
      Crushed dried red peppers
  3 to 4 cups cauliflowerets
  ¾ cup vegetable or chicken broth
  3 ounces enokis, stems trimmed
  1 cup fresh or frozen peas
  1 cup chopped, seeded tomatoes
  2 tablespoons chopped cilantro

In large skillet, melt butter over moderate heat. Add shiitakes, onion, curry powder, and red pepper. Cook, stirring frequently, 8 to 10 minutes or until onion is soft.

Add cauliflowerets and broth, cover and cook until cauliflower is tender, about 15 minutes. Stir in enokis, peas, and tomato and cook until heated through. Transfer to serving dish and sprinkle with cilantro.

Serves 6.

WILD RICE WITH OYSTER MUSHROOMS

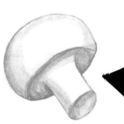

½ cup wild rice, rinsed and drained
1½ cups chicken broth
3 tablespoons butter
½ pound small oyster mushrooms
¼ cup pine nuts
2 tablespoons chopped chives
1 teaspoon chopped fresh thyme
Coarse salt and freshly ground pepper

In medium saucepan, bring rice and broth to boil. Cover, reduce heat, and simmer 35 to 45 minutes.

Meanwhile, in large skillet, melt butter over moderate heat. Add mushrooms and pine nuts and cook, stirring frequently, 10 minutes. Stir in chives and thyme and cook 5 minutes longer. Add to cooked rice and heat through. Season to taste with salt and pepper.

Serves 4.

TRATTORIA POTATOES

1½ pounds baking potatoes
¼ cup olive oil
2 garlic cloves, minced
2 teaspoons chopped fresh sage
½ cup duxelles (see p. 92)
  Coarse salt and freshly ground pepper
  Fresh sage leaves

Peel potatoes and cut into ½-inch cubes, dropping cubes into cold water to prevent browning.

In large skillet, heat oil over medium-high heat. Drain and pat potatoes dry and add to skillet. Stir to coat with oil. Stir in garlic and sage, reduce heat to low, and cover and cook until tender, about 15 minutes, stirring occasionally.

Uncover, increase heat to high, add duxelles and cook, stirring frequently, 5 minutes. Season to taste with salt and pepper. Transfer to serving dish and garnish with sage leaves.

Serves 6.

FOUR-MUSHROOM SAUTÉ

6 tablespoons butter
3 shallots, chopped
8 ounces medium-large domestic mushrooms
2 ounces shiitakes, sliced thickly
2 ounces oyster mushrooms
2 ounces enoki
   Coarse salt and freshly ground pepper

In large skillet, melt butter over medium-high heat. Add shallots and sauté until soft. Add domestic, shiitake, and oyster mushrooms and cook, tossing frequently, 3 minutes. Add enokis and cook 1 minute longer. Season to taste with salt and pepper.

Serves 4.

MOREL & CHESTNUT TURKEY STUFFING

3 ounces dried morels
1 cup hot chicken broth
¼ cup butter
3 onions, chopped
4 celery ribs, chopped
3 garlic cloves, minced
¼ cup chopped fresh parsley
2 teaspoons chopped fresh sage
2 teaspoons chopped fresh thyme
8 cups bread cubes or 2 (8-ounce) packages
   unseasoned stuffing mix
1 pound chestnuts, shelled, peeled, and quartered
   Coarse salt and freshly ground pepper

In bowl, soak morels in chicken broth 15 minutes. Remove mushrooms and squeeze out any excess broth. Strain broth and reserve with mushrooms.

In large skillet, melt butter over moderate heat. Add onions and celery and cook, stirring frequently, until onion is soft. Stir in garlic, parsley, sage, thyme, and mushrooms and cook, stirring frequently, 5 minutes longer.

In large bowl, combine bread cubes with chestnuts. Add mushroom mixture and reserved broth. Toss until bread is evenly moistened and season to taste with salt and pepper.

Use to stuff 12- to 15-pound turkey. Wrap any remaining stuffing in foil and refrigerate. Cook foil-wrapped stuffing alongside turkey during last hour of roasting.

Makes about 12 cups.

CONTENTS

MUSHROOMS
IN THE
MAINSTREAM

STUFFED CHICKEN BREASTS WITH CHANTERELLES

Sautéed chanterelles with a touch of garlic and lemon juice make a simple sauce for pan-fried chicken.

4 boneless chicken breast halves
4 slices thinly sliced prosciutto
  Salt and black pepper
2 tablespoons olive oil
1 tablespoon butter
1 garlic clove, minced
1/2 pound chanterelles, cleaned and sliced
  Juice of 1/2 lemon
1/4 cup chopped fresh Italian parsley

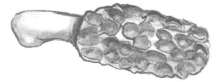

Preheat oven to 250 degrees F.

Pound chicken breasts to flatten. Insert finger
between skin and meat to loosen and insert slice of
prosciutto in each. Season generously with salt
and pepper.

Heat oil and butter in large skillet, preferably
nonstick, over high heat. Sauté the chicken until lightly
browned on both sides, about 3 minutes per side.
Transfer to an ovenproof platter and keep warm in oven.

Reduce heat in pan to medium-low and quickly fry
garlic, being careful not to burn. Add mushrooms and
sauté over medium heat, shaking pan frequently,
about 5 minutes. Sprinkle lemon juice and parsley
and remove from heat. Scatter mushroom
mixture over chicken and serve.

Serves 4.

WILD TURKEY LOAF

3 tablespoons olive oil
1 tablespoon minced garlic
1 onion, chopped
4 ounces oyster mushrooms, roughly chopped
6 ounces domestic mushrooms, roughly chopped
1 tablespoon tomato paste
1¼ pound ground turkey
1 egg, beaten
¾ cup bread crumbs
¼ cup chopped fresh oregano
Salt and freshly ground pepper

Heat 2 tablespoons of olive oil in large skillet over medium heat. Cook garlic and onions until soft, about 5 minutes. Add remaining oil and mushrooms and turn heat to high. Cook until mushrooms give off their liquid. Stir in tomato paste and continue cooking until moisture evaporates. Remove from heat.

Preheat oven to 350 degrees F. Place turkey in mixing bowl and break up with fork. Add egg, bread crumbs, oregano, 1/2 teaspoon salt and black pepper, and mushroom mixture. Mix well. Pat mixture into 9 by 5 by 3-inch loaf pan and smooth top. Bake 50 to 60 minutes, until top is browned and edges pull away from pan. Cool slightly and cut in slices to serve.

Serves 6.

CHICKEN WITH CORN & WILD MUSHROOMS

Here is an exceptional light, clear stir-fry of chicken with three traditional Chinese mushrooms: straw, oyster, and dried shiitake or black mushrooms.

3/4 pound skinless, boneless chicken breast,
   cut in 1/2-inch cubes
   Salt and pepper
1/4 cup peanut oil
 2 garlic cloves, minced
 3 scallions, chopped
 1 cup fresh corn kernels
 2 ounces dried Chinese black mushrooms or shiitakes,
   soaked in hot water 15 minutes, stemmed and quartered
 4 ounces oyster mushrooms, in bite-sized pieces
 2 ounces canned Chinese straw mushrooms, rinsed
 3 tablespoons chicken broth
 2 teaspoons soy sauce
 1 teaspoon dry sherry
1/4 teaspoon sugar

Sprinkle chicken with salt and pepper.

Heat 2 tablespoons oil in wok or large skillet over high heat. Briefly stir-fry chicken just until opaque, about 2 minutes. Transfer to platter.

Heat remaining oil in same pan. Stir-fry garlic and scallions less than a minute. Add corn and all the mushrooms and stir-fry briefly. Add remaining ingredients and reserved chicken. Cook, stirring and tossing, until everything is coated and crisp-cooked, about 3 minutes. Serve hot.

Serves 4.

SHIITAKES

Shiitakes, also known as Chinese Black and Black Forest mushrooms, are the most popular cultivated wild mushroom in America. As a staple of Chinese cooking, they have long been available in dried form in American supermarkets, but now the fresh form is also available in many produce sections. The Japanese have been cultivating shiitakes for 2,000 years.

The beige to brown, thin-stemmed, musky-smelling shiitake is available all year round. Fresh ones need never be discarded, as they are delicious as they dry out. Many people prefer the more intense flavor of dried shiitakes to fresh. Shiitake stems are too tough to eat and should always be removed.

WILD MUSHROOM LASAGNE

4 tablespoons olive oil
3 garlic cloves, minced
2 onions, thinly sliced
1 pound wild mushrooms, such as porcini, oyster, shiitake, morel, or a mixture
1/4 cup chopped Italian parsley
1 tablespoon chopped fresh thyme
1/2 cup dry Marsala wine
Coarse salt and freshly ground pepper
1/4 cup butter
1/4 cup all-purpose flour
1/8 teaspoon ground nutmeg
1 cup beef or vegetable broth
1 cup milk
2 cups shredded fontina
12 spinach lasagne noodles
1 cup shredded mozzarella
1 cup grated Parmesan

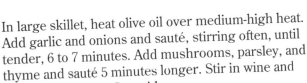

In large skillet, heat olive oil over medium-high heat. Add garlic and onions and sauté, stirring often, until tender, 6 to 7 minutes. Add mushrooms, parsley, and thyme and sauté 5 minutes longer. Stir in wine and simmer 5 minutes. Set aside.

In large saucepan, melt butter over medium heat. Blend in flour and nutmeg. Cook and stir until bubbly. Gradually stir in broth and milk. Cook and stir until sauce boils and thickens slightly. Stir in fontina and cook just until melted.

Preheat oven to 375 degrees F. In bottom of 12 by 8-inch baking dish arrange 1/3 of the lasagne noodles in single layer. Spread with 1/4 of the mushroom mixture and 1/4 of the sauce. Repeat layers with remaining noodles, mushroom mixture, and sauce, ending with sauce. Sprinkle with mozzarella and Parmesan. Cover with foil and bake 30 minutes. Remove foil and bake 10 minutes longer. Cut into squares to serve.

Serves 6 to 8.

FETTUCINE WITH WILD MUSHROOMS

What to eat when satisfaction and flavor take precedence over lowering your cholesterol.

6 tablespoons butter
1 small onion, finely chopped
4 garlic cloves, minced
12 ounces mixed oyster mushrooms and shiitakes (caps only), roughly chopped
Salt and pepper
1 cup heavy cream
2 tablespoons fresh chopped thyme
2 tablespoons lemon juice
2 teaspoons soy sauce
1 pound fettucine, cooked and drained

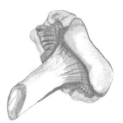

Melt butter in large skillet over medium heat. Cook onions, garlic, salt, and pepper until lightly golden. Add mushrooms, turn up heat, and cook, stirring and tossing frequently, until soft, about 2 minutes. Pour in cream and herbs and boil for 5 minutes to thicken. Stir in lemon juice and soy sauce and remove from heat.

Pour sauce over hot pasta and toss well. Serve with Parmesan cheese, if desired.

Serves 4.

FRESH VERSUS DRIED

Drying is a time-honored way to preserve wild mushrooms. Dried porcini, morels, and cloud ears are much easier to come by then the fresh variety and are just as prized. To reconstitute, soak in hot tap water 15 to 30 minutes, depending on the mushrooms' size, and then squeeze out any excess water before cooking. The soaking liquid can be strained and used as an addition to stocks and stews. Dried mushrooms can be stored in a plastic bag in a cool, dry place or frozen indefinitely. One ounce dried mushrooms reconstitutes to 7 to 10 ounces.

YAKITORI CHICKEN WITH SHIITAKES

¼ cup dry sherry
¼ cup soy sauce
2 tablespoons sesame oil
1 teaspoon minced fresh ginger
¼ teaspoon cayenne
2 pounds skinless, boneless chicken breasts
18 green onions, trimmed to 2 inches, including white part
18 medium shiitake mushrooms

In bowl, combine sherry, soy sauce, sesame oil, ginger, and cayenne for marinade.

Cut chicken into bite-sized pieces and place in bowl with green onions. Pour ¼ cup marinade mixture over chicken and toss to coat. Let stand 1 hour or refrigerate overnight.

When ready to grill, dip mushrooms in remaining marinade. Thread on skewers with chicken and onions. Place skewers on grill about 6 inches from coals and cook 10 to 12 minutes, turning several times. Serve with remaining marinade as dipping sauce.

Serves 6.

PENNE WITH CREMINI-TOMATO SAUCE

2 tablespoons olive oil
4 garlic cloves, crushed
1 onion, chopped
1 pound cremini, stemmed and coarsely chopped
1/3 cup chopped fresh Italian parsley
1 dried hot red pepper, crushed
1 (1-pound, 12-ounce) can crushed Italian tomatoes
   Coarse salt
1 pound penne, cooked and drained
1/2 cup grated fresh Parmesan

In large skillet, heat oil over medium-high heat. Add garlic and onion and cook just until soft, stirring frequently. Stir in mushrooms and cook 10 minutes more, stirring frequently. Stir in parsley, hot pepper, and tomatoes. Bring to boil then reduce heat and simmer 10 minutes. Season to taste with salt. Spoon sauce over hot penne and serve with Parmesan.

Serves 6.

WILD MUSHROOM PIZZA

2 tablespoons olive oil
2 shallots, thinly sliced
2 teaspoons minced garlic
4 ounces wild mushrooms, such as shiitake caps, oyster mushrooms, or chanterelles, thinly sliced
2 small Boboli pizza crusts
1 cup grated mozzarella cheese
8 fresh oregano or basil leaves, roughly chopped
1/2 cup grated Parmesan cheese

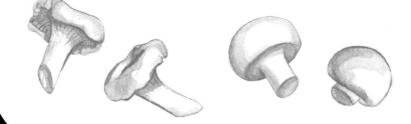

Preheat oven to 450 degrees F.
Heat olive oil in small skillet over medium-high heat. Sauté shallots and garlic 1 minute. Add mushrooms, stirring frequently, and cook just to soften, 1 to 2 minutes longer. Remove from heat.

Arrange pizza crusts on baking sheet. Sprinkle each with mozzarella, leaving crust bare along edges. Divide mushroom mixture and spread over each. Scatter basil or oregano on top, sprinkle with Parmesan, and bake 8 to 10 minutes, until cheese melts.

Serves 2.

CLOUD, WOOD, OR JEW'S EAR

These dried Chinese mushrooms are the crinkly, black, gelatinous chewy bits that carry the sauce and add texture to dishes like mu shu pork and hot and sour soup. Reconstitute as any dried mushroom and cut into small pieces.

PORCINI RISOTTO

This traditional Italian dish of plump risotto and fragrant porcini is wonderful winter food.

2 ounces dried porcini mushrooms
1 (14.5-ounce) can beef broth
4 tablespoons butter
1 onion, diced
1 garlic clove, minced
2 cups Arborio rice
1/2 cup dry white wine
3/4 cup grated Parmesan

Soak mushrooms in enough hot water to cover for 30 minutes. Lift out, chop into large pieces, and reserve. Strain soaking liquid and reserve.

Combine soaking liquid, beef broth, and enough water to make 6 cups total in another saucepan and bring to low boil.

In heavy medium-sized saucepan, melt 2 tablespoons butter over medium-low heat. Sauté onion and garlic until soft. Add rice, stirring to evenly coat, and cook about 2 minutes longer. Add wine and cook until pan is nearly dry. Stir in mushrooms along with 1 cup warm broth mixture.

Continue adding warm broth, 1/2 cup at a time, stirring constantly, until all liquid is absorbed. Risotto should cook at constant simmer until al dente, about 20 minutes. Remove from heat, stir in remaining butter and Parmesan, cover, and let sit 10 minutes. Serve hot.

Serves 6.

GRILLED LAMB WILD MUSHROOM SALAD

This winter salad delivers the sort of deep, country flavors you don't expect from such a quickly cooked dish. It makes a nice choice for a romantic dinner for two, with a loaf of crusty French bread and a bottle of red wine.

2 medium Yukon gold potatoes, washed
2 ounces young green beans, trimmed
1 bunch watercress, washed, dried, and trimmed
1 teaspoon puréed garlic
2 tablespoons lemon juice
3 tablespoons olive oil
2 small lamb rib chops
   Olive oil and mustard for coating
   Coarse salt and freshly ground pepper
4 ounces shiitake, pieds de moutons, or chicken
   of the woods mushrooms, trimmed, cleaned,
   and roughly chopped

Place potatoes in small pot with enough water to cover. Bring to boil and cook until just done, about 20 minutes. Drain, rinse with cold water, and pat dry. In another pot, blanch green beans 2 minutes. Drain, let cool in cold water, and pat dry.

Preheat broiler or grill. Place watercress in bowl. Whisk together 1/2 teaspoon garlic, lemon juice, olive oil, and salt and pepper to taste to make dressing. Pour half over watercress, toss to coat and set aside. Meanwhile rub lamb chops all over with olive oil, mustard, salt, and pepper. Grill or broil 2 minutes per side and remove from heat.

In small skillet heat enough oil to thinly coat pan. Briefly sauté 1/2 teaspoon garlic just to release aroma. Add mushrooms and sauté over high heat 1 minute. Then reduce heat to medium low and cook until pan is nearly dry. Season with salt and pepper.

To serve, divide watercress and arrange bed of greens in center of each serving plate. Place a chop along each rim, followed by a pile of green beans, a thinly sliced potato and a pile of mushrooms. Drizzle remaining dressing over beans, potato and chop. Serve immediately.

Serves 2.

VEAL SCALOPPINE WITH CHANTERELLES

Veal really benefits from the added flavor of rich chanterelles.

1 pound thinly sliced veal scallops
Flour
Salt and freshly ground pepper
5 tablespoons butter
1 tablespoon olive oil
¼ cup minced shallots or onion
1 garlic clove, minced
½ pound chanterelles, stems trimmed and chopped
½ cup dry white wine
3 tablespoons chopped fresh Italian parsley

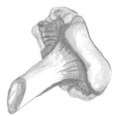

Lightly coat veal with flour and pat off excess. Season all over with salt and pepper. Melt 1 tablespoon of butter and oil together in large skillet over medium-high heat. Sauté scallops in batches, less than 1 minute per side, and transfer to platter.

Add 1 tablespoon butter to pan and reduce heat to medium. Cook onion or shallots and garlic until soft. Add mushrooms, turn up heat, and cook another 5 minutes, stirring frequently. Pour in wine and cook until liquid is reduced to about 2 tablespoons. Reduce heat to low. Cut remaining butter into pieces and swirl into pan one at a time until melted. Stir in parsley and return scallops to pan. Cook a minute or so longer, turning veal to heat through, and serve.

Serves 4.

There are two schools of mushroom sautéers. Some believe in sautéing fast to seal in moisture and retain some bite. Others favor sautéing slowly to concentrate flavor and soften texture. We refuse to take sides.

VEAL CHOPS WITH MOREL CREAM

1 ounce dried morels
2 cups reduced-sodium chicken broth
½ cup dry white wine
2 tablespoons chopped shallots
1 cup whipping cream
Coarse salt and freshly ground pepper
4 (¾-inch) veal chops
Olive oil
1 tablespoon chopped fresh Italian parsley

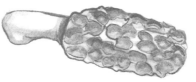

In small bowl soak morels 10 minutes in enough warm water just to cover. Remove from soaking liquid and squeeze, removing as much moisture as possible. Strain soaking liquid through fine sieve lined with clean cloth. Set morels aside and reserve liquid.

In saucepan, combine strained soaking liquid, wine, and shallots. Bring to boil and cook until liquid is reduced to about 1/3 cup. Stir in cream and morels. Return to boil and cook until slightly thickened. Season to taste with salt and pepper. Keep warm.

Rub veal chops liberally with olive oil. Grill over medium-hot coals about 6 minutes per side. Serve topped with morel sauce and sprinkled with parsley.

Serves 4.

With their long, narrow honeycomb caps, morels look distinctly unmushroomlike. The flavor, however, is pure sweet woods—similar enough to pass for truffles in a well-turned cream sauce. They are available at specialty stores and farmer's markets, at a steep price, mostly in dried form.

MUSHROOM-STUFFED PEPPER STEAK

2 pounds flank steak
3 garlic cloves, thinly sliced
2 tablespoons cracked black pepper
2 teaspoons chopped fresh rosemary
2 teaspoons chopped fresh Italian parsley
1/2 cup dry red wine
1/4 cup soy sauce
3 tablespoons butter
1 pound cremini or domestic mushrooms, sliced
5 shallots, chopped
1 cup beef broth

Place steak, fat side down, in 13 by 9-inch baking pan. Scatter garlic slices over meat and sprinkle with 1 tablespoon of pepper and all of the rosemary and parsley. Rub seasonings into meat. Mix wine and soy sauce and pour over steak. Cover and marinate at least 1 hour at room temperature or overnight in refrigerator.

Preheat oven to 350 degrees F. In large skillet, melt butter over medium-high heat. Add mushrooms and shallots and cook, stirring frequently, 8 to 10 minutes or until liquid has evaporated and mushrooms are brown.

Lift meat from marinade and lay flat. Spread mushrooms over meat to within 1 inch of edges. Roll meat up and tie in 3 places with kitchen string. Rub surface with remaining pepper. Return to pan with marinade, cover with foil, and bake 2 hours or until meat is tender when tested with fork. Transfer meat to platter and cover with foil. Skim and discard fat from liquid in pan. Pour liquid into saucepan and stir in beef broth. Bring to boil and cook until reduced to 1 cup.

To serve, remove string from meat and slice. Serve with hot sauce.

Serves 6.

MUSHROOM STEAK SANDWICH

5 (1-inch-thick) slices French bread
4 teaspoons butter
3 garlic cloves, minced
1 cup beef broth
1 pound cremini or domestic mushrooms, quartered
1 teaspoon chopped fresh thyme
2 tablespoons chopped fresh Italian parsley
  Coarse salt and freshly ground pepper
4 (4- to 6-ounce) steaks, grilled as desired

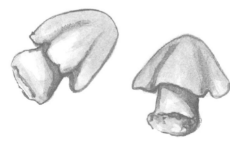

Preheat broiler.

Cut 1 bread slice into cubes and process in blender to make crumbs. Set aside.

Lightly toast both sides of 4 remaining bread slices. Spread butter mixed with 1/3 garlic on one side of each. Cook under broiler until browned. Set aside.

In skillet, bring broth, mushrooms, and remaining garlic to boil. Reduce heat, cover, and simmer about 5 minutes. Stir crumbs, thyme, and parsley into mushroom mixture and cook over high heat, stirring frequently, until liquid has evaporated. Season to taste with salt and pepper. To serve, top each toasted bread slice with steak and mushrooms.

Serves 4.

A chef's trick to intensify flavor and save money is to combine a small proportion of wild to domestic mushrooms to boost mushroom flavor.

MIXED MUSHROOM STEW

2 pounds plum tomatoes
3 tablespoons olive oil
1/2 pound domestic mushrooms, quartered
1/2 pound oyster mushrooms, halved
1/4 pound porcini mushrooms, thickly sliced
6 large shallots, chopped
2 tablespoons chopped sun-dried tomatoes
1 tablespoon chopped fresh thyme
1 bay leaf
1 cup vegetable or beef broth
1/2 cup dry red wine
Coarse salt and freshly ground pepper
Chopped fresh Italian parsley or fresh thyme sprigs
Freshly grated Parmesan (optional)

Roast tomatoes over gas flame or cook under hot broiler, turning frequently, until blackened all over. When cool enough to handle, peel, cut in halves, and seed. Chop roughly and set aside.

In large pot, heat oil over medium high heat. Add mushrooms and shallots and cook, stirring frequently, 8 to 10 minutes or until mushrooms are browned and shallots are soft. Stir in sun-dried tomatoes, thyme, bay leaf, broth, wine, and reserved tomatoes and bring to boil. Reduce heat and simmer, uncovered, 20 minutes, stirring occasionally. Season to taste with salt and pepper.

Serve in bowls sprinkled with parsley and Parmesan, if desired.

Serves 4 to 6.

STEAMED SEABASS WITH SHIITAKES

- 3 tablespoons soy sauce
- 2 teaspoons sesame oil
- 1 tablespoon fermented black beans, rinsed
- 1 teaspoon sugar
- 1 garlic clove, chopped
- 1 (½-inch) slice ginger, chopped
- 1 dried hot red chile, seeded and crumbled
- 4 seabass fillets, cut ¾- to 1-inch thick
- 3 to 4 ounces shiitakes (caps only), sliced
  Cilantro sprigs

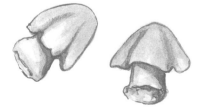

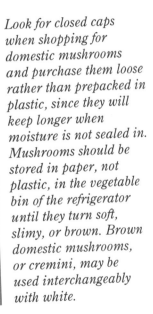

In blender combine soy sauce, sesame oil, black beans, sugar, garlic, ginger, and chile and process to blend.

Place fish in single layer on heat-proof plate that fits in steamer. Pour seasoning mixture over fish and scatter with mushrooms. Place plate in steamer over simmering water. Cover and steam over medium-high heat 10 minutes or until fish is done. Transfer fish pieces to dinner plates and top with mushrooms and sauce. Garnish with cilantro.

Serves 4.

Look for closed caps when shopping for domestic mushrooms and purchase them loose rather than prepacked in plastic, since they will keep longer when moisture is not sealed in. Mushrooms should be stored in paper, not plastic, in the vegetable bin of the refrigerator until they turn soft, slimy, or brown. Brown domestic mushrooms, or cremini, may be used interchangeably with white.

STIR-FRIED SQUID WITH CHINESE TREE EARS

3/4 pound dried Chinese tree ears
1 teaspoon sugar
2 teaspoon cornstarch
1 tablespoon soy sauce
1 tablespoon oyster sauce
3/4 cup chicken broth
3 tablespoons vegetable oil
2 slices fresh ginger
2 garlic cloves, lightly crushed
1 dried hot red pepper, lightly crushed
3/4 pound squid rings
6 green onions, cut into 1 1/2-inch lengths
Hot cooked rice or pan-fried noodles

Place tree ears in bowl with enough warm water to cover. Let stand 30 minutes. Drain. Remove tough stems and slice 1/2-inch thick. Set aside.

In small bowl, blend sugar with cornstarch. Stir in soy sauce, oyster sauce, and chicken broth. Set aside.

Heat wok over high heat, then pour in oil. When hot, add ginger, garlic, and dried pepper. Stir-fry 30 seconds. Remove and discard flavorings. Add squid and stir-fry 1 minute. Set aside.

Add tree ears and stir-fry 1 minute. Return squid to pan along with green onions and stir-fry 1 minute longer. Swirl broth mixture and add to wok. Bring to boil and cook, stirring, until thickened and clear. Serve over rice or noodles.

Serves 4 to 6.

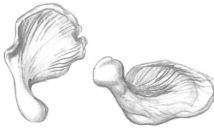

CONTENTS

MUSHROOM STANDARDS

DUXELLES

4 tablespoons unsalted butter
3 cups finely chopped domestic mushrooms
5 shallots, minced
1/2 teaspoon coarse salt
1/4 teaspoon freshly ground pepper

In skillet, melt butter over medium-high heat. Add mushrooms, shallots, salt, and pepper and cook, stirring frequently, 10 to 15 minutes or until liquid has evaporated. Can be refrigerated up to 10 days. Use to season soups, stews, and sauces or as topping for vegetables, meats, chicken, or fish.

Makes about 1 cup.

PORCINI BUTTER

1 ounce dried porcini
1 cup hot chicken or beef broth
1/2 cup unsalted butter
  Coarse salt and freshly ground pepper

In small bowl, combine porcini and broth and let stand 30 minutes. Drain mushrooms, reserving broth, and place in food processor. Strain broth and reduce over medium heat to 3 to 4 tablespoons. Add to mushrooms and process to purée. Add butter and process to blend. Transfer to 6-ounce ramekin or other serving dish. Use butter as spread or topping for hot vegetables, meats, chicken, or fish.

Makes about 3/4 cup.

SPICY PICKLED SHIITAKES

6 cups water
6 tablespoons coarse salt
1½ pounds medium shiitakes, stems trimmed and caps halved
2 cups rice vinegar
4 teaspoons sesame oil
4 garlic cloves, peeled
4 tiny hot dried red peppers

Sterilize 4 (8-ounce) jars and lids.

In saucepan, combine water and salt. Add shiitakes, bring to simmer, cover, and cook 5 minutes. Drain.

In saucepan, heat vinegar and oil to boiling. Add shiitakes and simmer, uncovered, 5 minutes. With slotted spoon, remove mushrooms and pack into prepared jars. Place 1 garlic clove and 1 dried pepper in each jar.

Return vinegar to boil and pour into jars, filling to within 1/8 inch of top. Seal and store in refrigerator 2 to 3 weeks before serving.

Makes 4 (8-ounce) jars.

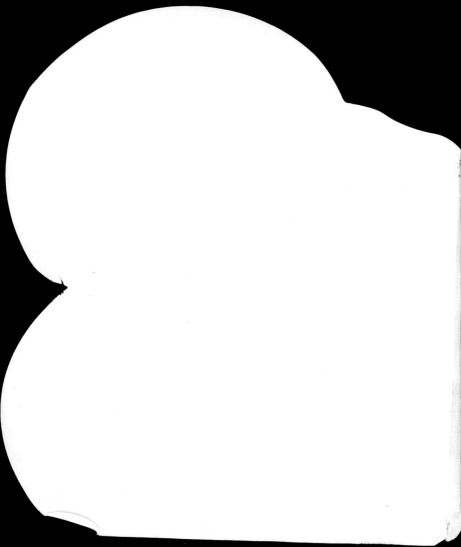

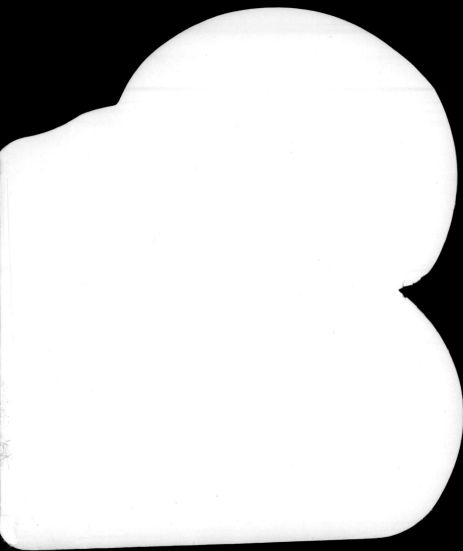

$4.95

CELESTIAL ARTS

Berkeley, Californ

ISBN 0-89087-727-0

EAN

9 780890 877272

another idea from becker&

W8-CCW-735